The Prophet's Pond ﷺ

Discover Kawthar

Your Meeting Place with Muhammad ﷺ

First published in the United Kingdom in 1437 AH (2015 CE) by
Learning Roots Ltd.
Unit 6, TGEC, Town Hall Approach Road, London, N15 4RX
www.learningroots.com

Copyright © Learning Roots 2023
Authored by Zaheer Khatri.
Illustrations commissioned by Learning Roots.
Layout and design by Jannah Haque.

Acknowledgments
The publisher thanks Allah, Lord of the Worlds, for making this publication possible.

British Library Cataloging in Publication Data
A CIP catalogue record for this book is available from the British Library.

Printed and bound by in Turkey.
ISBN: 978-1-915381-21-7 (Paperback Edition)

فَاصْبِرُوا حَتَّى تَلْقَوْنِي عَلَى الحَوْضِ

"Remain patient until you meet me by the pond."

*This story was inspired by the words of the Messenger of Allah, Muhammad ﷺ,
as narrated in Saheeh Al-Bukhari.*

"Mummy," said Zayd,
"I'm meeting someone by a special pond.
It's someone of whom I'm most fond.
But it may be a little hard to find,
so please help me, if you'd be so kind."

"Why of course," said Mummy. "I don't mind.
A pond shouldn't be too hard to find."

So they set off, walking along,
through a park, and way beyond,
until they stumbled upon...

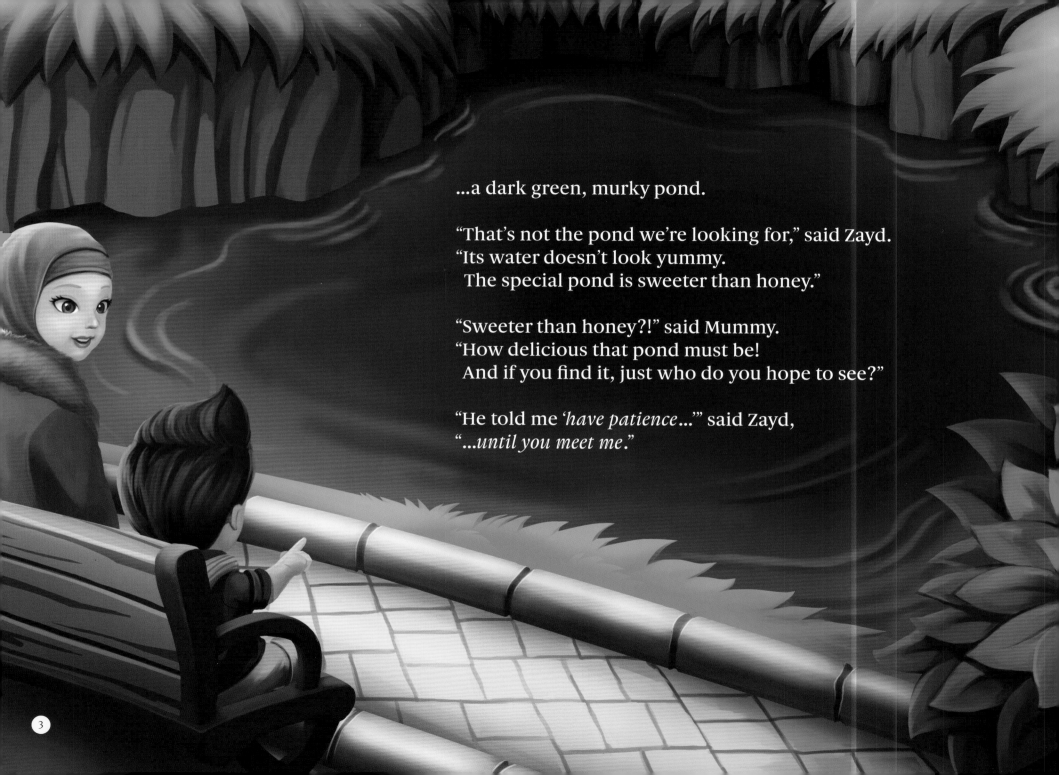

...a dark green, murky pond.

"That's not the pond we're looking for," said Zayd.
"Its water doesn't look yummy.
 The special pond is sweeter than honey."

"Sweeter than honey?!" said Mummy.
"How delicious that pond must be!
 And if you find it, just who do you hope to see?"

"He told me *'have patience...'*" said Zayd,
"*...until you meet me.*"

So they marched on,
crossing a meadow,
and way beyond,
until they stumbled upon...

...a rich, thick, sticky pond.

"No that can't be it," said Zayd.
"Its colour is dark like the night.
 The special pond is brighter than milk-white."

"Brighter than milk-white?!" said Mummy.
"How delightful that pond must be!
 And if you find it, just who do you hope to see?"

"He told me *'have patience...'*" said Zayd,
"*...until you meet me.*"

So they rambled on,
into a forest,
and way beyond,
until they stumbled upon...

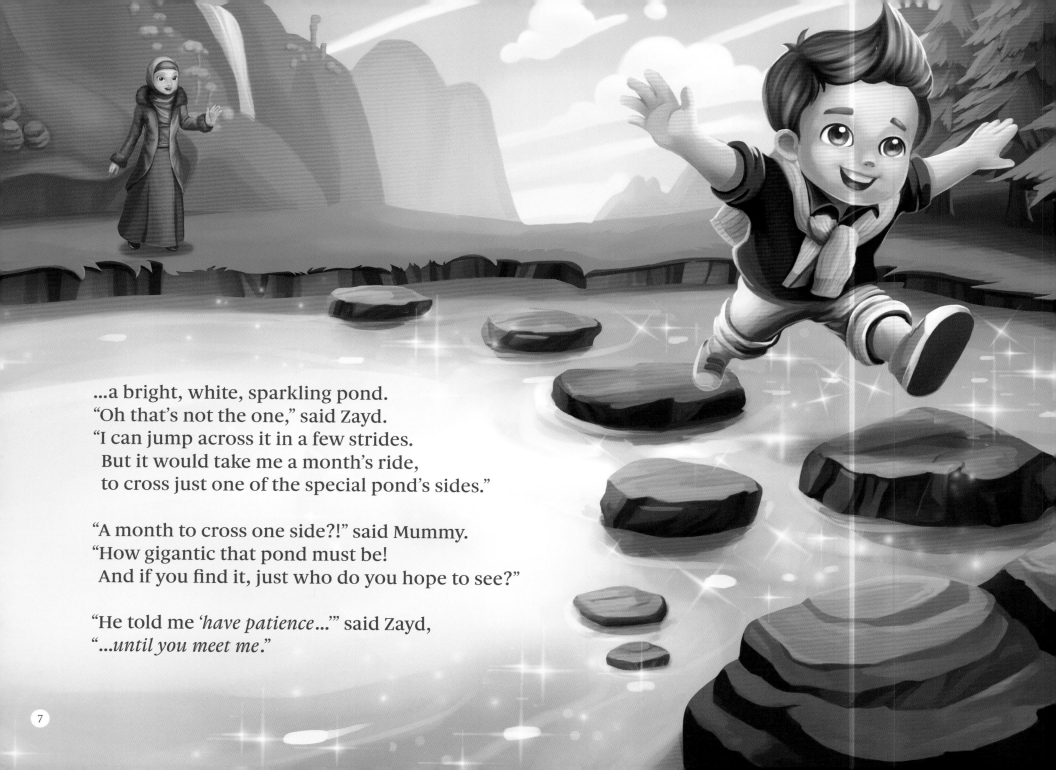

...a bright, white, sparkling pond.
"Oh that's not the one," said Zayd.
"I can jump across it in a few strides.
 But it would take me a month's ride,
 to cross just one of the special pond's sides."

"A month to cross one side?!" said Mummy.
"How gigantic that pond must be!
 And if you find it, just who do you hope to see?"

"He told me *'have patience...'*" said Zayd,
"*...until you meet me.*"

So they trekked on,
up a mountain,
and way beyond,
until they stumbled upon...

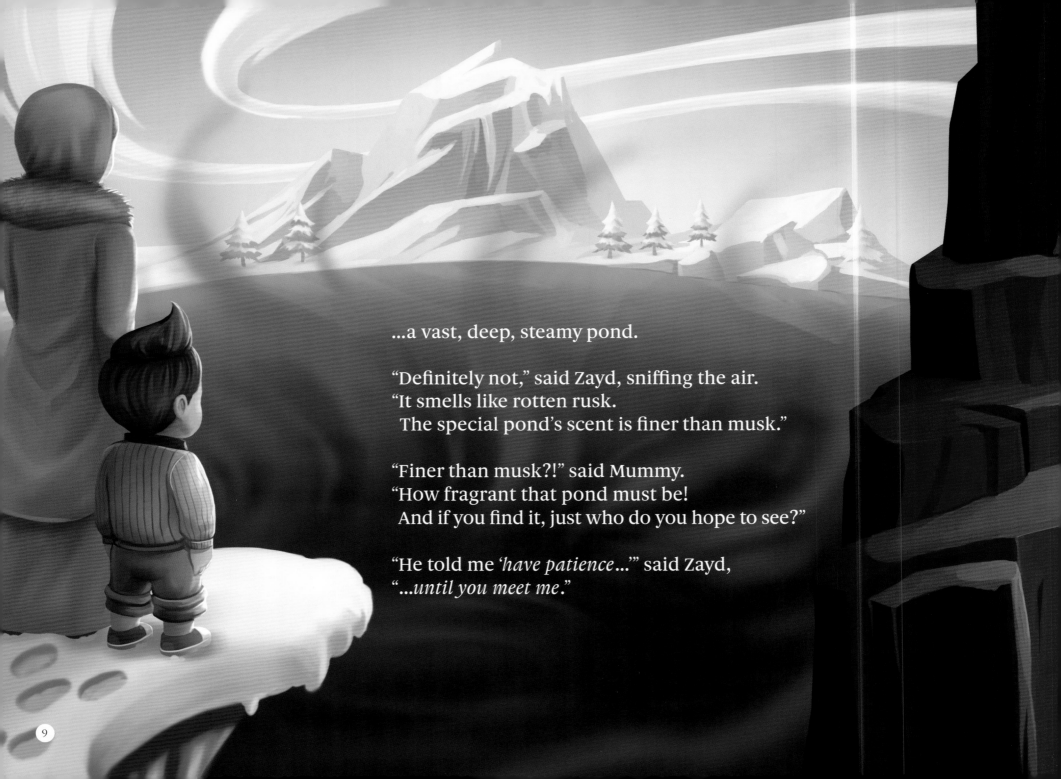

...a vast, deep, steamy pond.

"Definitely not," said Zayd, sniffing the air.
"It smells like rotten rusk.
 The special pond's scent is finer than musk."

"Finer than musk?!" said Mummy.
"How fragrant that pond must be!
 And if you find it, just who do you hope to see?"

"He told me *'have patience...'*" said Zayd,
"*...until you meet me.*"

So they roamed on,
across a valley,
and way beyond,
until they stumbled upon...

10

...a fine, sandy, scented pond.

"Not at all," said Zayd, feeling his throat turning dry.
"There are no cups here for me to try.
 But the special pond is sprinkled with cups;
 More cups than the stars in the sky."

"More cups than the stars in the sky?!" said Mummy.
"What a sight that pond must be!
 And if you find it, just who do you hope to see?"

"He told me 'have patience...'" said Zayd,
"...until you meet me."

So they sailed on,
down a river,
and way beyond,
until they stumbled upon...

...a freshwater, speckled pond.

"I'm afraid not," said Zayd,
  as he scooped its water up to his lips.
"I still feel thirsty after these sips.
  But one taste of what the special pond contains,
  and I'll never ever feel thirsty again."

"Never ever feel thirsty again?!" said Mummy.
"How can that possibly be?!
  And if you find it, just who do you hope to see?"

"He told me *have patience...*" said Zayd,
"*...until you meet me.*"

So they strolled on,
by a waterfall, and way beyond,
until they stumbled upon...

...a crystal-clear, icy pond.

"At last!" said Zayd. "A pond of ice!"
"*Alhamdulillah*," said Mummy.
"That should suffice."
"Not quite," said Zayd.
"The special pond is far more cold,
   and is fed by Paradise streams twofold;
   One stream of silver and the other of gold."

"Paradise streams of silver and gold?!"
   said Mummy with a little laughter.
"Why that's a pond from the hereafter!
   And now I know, just who you hope to see.
   But nonetheless, I'd like you to tell me!"

"Alright," said Zayd,
"since we've come so far...
   I hope to meet...

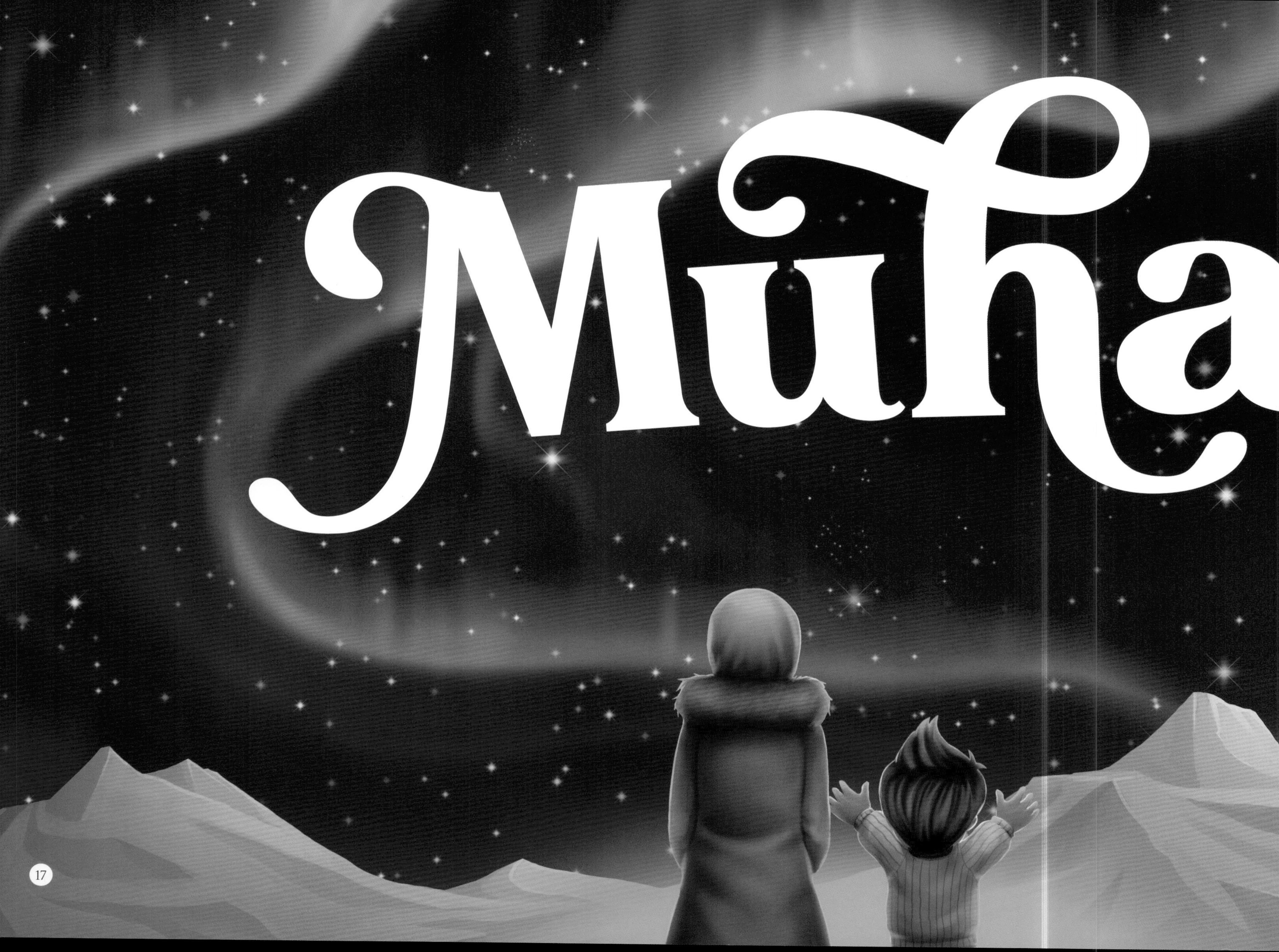
Muha

mmad ﷺ

The Messenger of Allah.

He's the one of whom I'm most fond.
He's the one I hope to meet by the special pond."

Mummy wiped the tears from her eyes.
"I pray he'll have in store for us a surprise.
When we meet him and over the Pond we all stand,
that he gives us its water with his own hand.

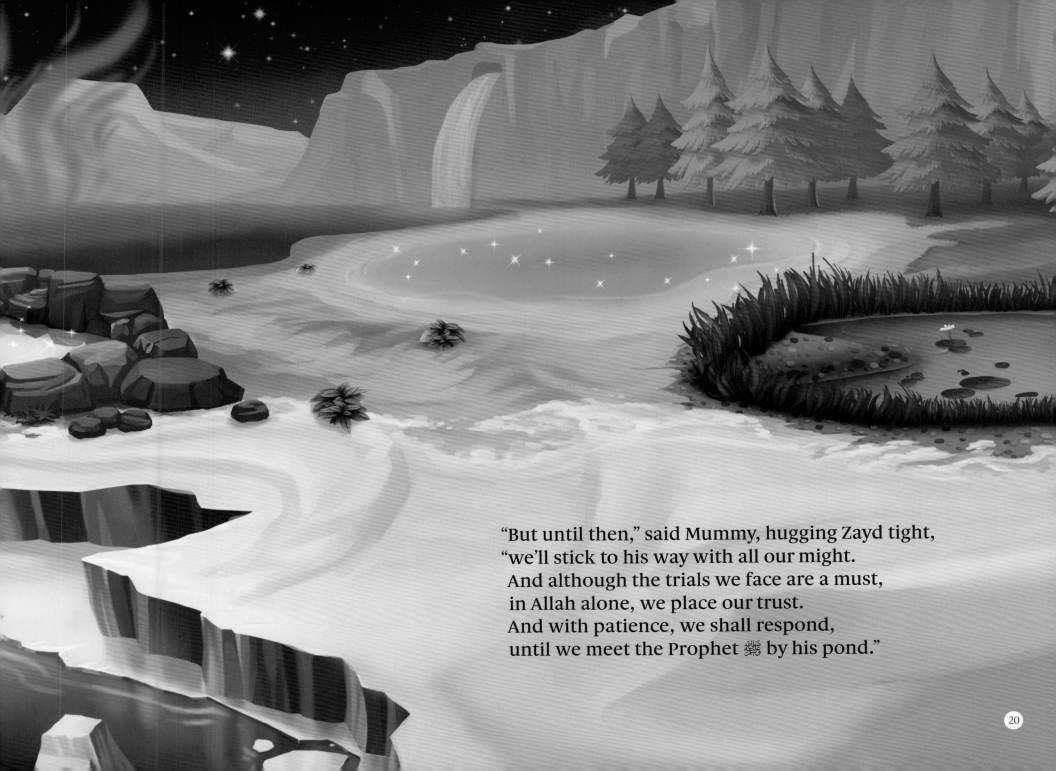

"But until then," said Mummy, hugging Zayd tight,
"we'll stick to his way with all our might.
And although the trials we face are a must,
in Allah alone, we place our trust.
And with patience, we shall respond,
until we meet the Prophet ﷺ by his pond."

References

قَالَ عَبْدُ اللَّهِ بْنُ عَمْرٍو قَالَ النَّبِيُّ صَلَّى اللَّهُ عَلَيْهِ وَسَلَّم
(حَوْضِي مَسِيرَةُ شَهْرٍ، مَاؤُهُ أَبْيَضُ مِنَ اللَّبَنِ، وَرِيحُهُ أَطْيَبُ
مِنَ الْمِسْكِ، وَكِيزَانُهُ كَنُجُومِ السَّمَاءِ، مَنْ شَرِبَ مِنْهَا فَلاَ
يَظْمَأُ أَبَدًا)

Narrated `Abdullah bin `Amr: The Prophet ﷺ said,
"My *Hawd* is (so large that it takes) a
month's journey (to cross it). Its water is
whiter than milk, and its smell is better
than musk, and its drinking cups are (as
numerous) as the (number of) stars in the
sky. Whoever drinks from it, will never
ever be thirsty again."

Saheeh Al-Bukhari

عَن ابن عُمَر رَضِيَ اللَّهُ عَنهُمَا أَن النَّبِيّ صَلَّى اللَّهُ عَلَيْهِ وَسَلَّم قَالَ: (حَوضِي كَمَا بَيْنَ عَدَن وَعَمَّان ,أَبْرَد مِنَ الثلْجِ، وَأَحْلَى مِنَ العَسَل وَأَطيَب رِيحاً مِنَ الْمِسكِ...)

Narrated `Abdullah bin `Amr: The Prophet ﷺ said,
"My *Hawd* is as vast (as the distance)
between Aden and Amman, it is colder
than ice, sweeter than honey, and better
in smell than musk..."

**Narrated by Imam Ahmad and At-Tabarani
with an authentic corroborated chain of narration.**

The Arabic word '*hawd*' has no single-word equivalent
in the English language. So while it could be described
as a pool or a vast basin, we have chosen the word
'pond' for convenience, with the realisation that
alternative translations may exist.

Ponder Over the Pond

How do you think Zayd first learnt about the special pond? (Look at the picture on page 1 for a clue).

Who did Zayd want to take along with him in his search for the special pond?

Who did Zayd hope to meet at the special pond?

How did Zayd's mother know in the end that the pond was from the hereafter and not from this world?

What was your favourite part of the story?

Can you describe the Prophet's ﷺ Pond?

Refer back to the story to fill in the blanks.

The Prophet's ﷺ Pond is sweeter than ▢▢▢▢, brighter than ▢▢▢▢ and is sprinkled with more ▢▢▢ than the ▢▢▢ in the ▢▢▢.

The Prophet's ﷺ Pond is fed by two streams from Paradise, one stream of ▢▢▢▢ and the other of ▢▢▢. It has a scent that is finer than ▢▢▢ and after you taste what the Prophet's ﷺ Pond contains, you'll never-ever feel ▢▢▢▢ again.